Animals Can Be Special Friends

By Dorothy Chlad

Illustrated by Lydia Halverson

CHILDRENS PRESS ™

CHICAGO

Library of Congress Cataloging in Publication Data

Chlad, Dorothy.
  Animals can be special friends.

  (Safety town)
  Summary: Brief text and illustrations describe some
of the rules for taking care of pets and treating animals
at the zoo and in the wild.
  1. Pets—Juvenile literature. 2. Animals—Juvenile
literature. [1. Pets. 2. Animals. 3. Safety]
I. Halverson, Lydia, ill. II. Title. III. Series:
Chlad, Dorothy. Safety town.
SF416.2.C49   1985   636.08'87   84-23300
ISBN O-516-O1978-3

Hi, my name is Amy
and this is my pet,
Prince!

We play and
have lots of fun!

5

Mom, dad, and I
teach Prince tricks!

We wash and brush
him!

When Prince eats, we
do not play with him or
tease him!

We take him to the
animal doctor for shots
to keep him well.

I take care of Prince.
When it is cold Prince
cannot stay outside
very long.

My friend, Brenda,
lives in the country. Her
pet's name is Dart.

Sometimes I ride Dart.

15

16

Then we feed and
clean him.

Some animals are fun
to have as pets.

fish

turtle

dog

bird

rabbit

gerbil

guinea pig

cat

19

NEVER pet, play with,
or feed an animal you
do not know.

NEVER tease or throw
anything at animals.

An animal that does not know you could bite or hurt you.

You can feed and
pet some animals at
the zoo.

When we go
camping, we see many
animals and birds.

We are careful when
we feed wild animals.
We watch them, but
never try to pet them.

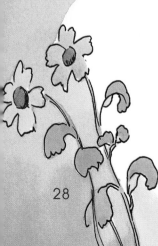

If you have a pet,
please take care of it.
Remember it must
be...fed every day,
cleaned and brushed,
and taken to the
animal doctor.

Remember these rules . . .

NEVER pet, play with, or feed an animal you do not know.

NEVER tease or throw anything at animals.

NEVER try to pet wild animals.

About the Author

Dorothy Chlad, founder of the total concept of Safety Town, is recognized internationally as a leader in Preschool/Early Childhood Safety Education. She has authored eight books on the program, and has conducted the only workshops dedicated to the concept. Under Mrs. Chlad's direction, the National Safety Town Center was founded to promote the program through community involvement.

She has presented the importance of safety education at local, state, and national safety and education conferences, such as National Community Education Association, National Safety Council, and the American Driver and Traffic Safety Education Association. She serves as a member of several national committees, such as the Highway Traffic Safety Division and the Educational Resources Division of National Safety Council. Chlad was an active participant at the Sixth International Conference on Safety Education.

Dorothy Chlad continues to serve as a consultant for State Departments of Safety and Education. She has also consulted for the TV program, "Sesame Street" and recently wrote this series of safety books for Childrens Press.

A participant of White House Conferences on safety, Dorothy Chlad has received numerous honors and awards including National Volunteer Activist and YMCA Career Woman of Achievement. In 1983, Dorothy Chlad was one of sixty people nationally to receive the **President's Volunteer Action Award** from President Reagan for twenty years of Safety Town efforts. She has also been selected for inclusion in the 14th Edition of **Who's Who of American Women.**

About the Artist

Lydia Halverson was born Lydia Geretti in midtown Manhattan. When she was two, her parents left New York and moved to Italy. Four years later her family returned to the United States and settled in the Chicago Area. Lydia attended the University of Illinois, graduating with a degree in fine arts. She worked as a graphic designer for many years before finally concentrating on book illustration.

Lydia lives with her husband and two cats in a suburb of Chicago and is active in several environmental organizations.